GABON 2016 HUMAN RIGHTS REPORT

Note: This report was updated 3/03/17; see Appendix F: Errata for more information.

EXECUTIVE SUMMARY

Gabon is a republic with a presidential form of government dominated by the Gabonese Democratic Party (PDG), which has held power since 1968. On August 31, the National Electoral Commission announced incumbent president Ali Bongo Ondimba defeated opponent Jean Ping in the August 27 election by a margin of less than 2 percent of the vote. Observers noted numerous irregularities, including a highly questionable vote count in Bongo's home province. The government forcibly dispersed violent demonstrations that followed the election. Observers characterized the 2011 legislative elections as generally free and fair, although some opposition parties boycotted them, citing the government's inability to provide for full transparency and prevent voter irregularities. PDG candidates won 114 of 120 seats in the National Assembly.

Civilian authorities generally maintained control over the security forces, but at times abuse and lapses of discipline occurred.

The most important human rights problems in the country were harsh prison conditions, lengthy pretrial detention, and arbitrary arrests, particularly following the disputed August 27 election.

Other serious human rights problems included: use of excessive force by police; police harassment and extortion of noncitizen Africans and refugees; an inefficient judiciary subject to government influence; restrictions on access to the internet and on freedom of assembly; government corruption; violence and societal discrimination against women, indigenous populations, lesbian, gay, bisexual, transgender, and intersex persons, and persons with HIV/AIDS; ritual killings; and trafficking in persons, including forced child labor.

The government took some steps to prosecute and punish officials convicted of abuses. Impunity remained a problem, however.

Section 1. Respect for the Integrity of the Person, Including Freedom from:

a. Arbitrary Deprivation of Life and other Unlawful or Politically Motivated

Killings

There were reports the government and its forces committed unlawful killings, particularly in the weeks following the election.

For example, nongovernmental organizations (NGOs) stated the government's use of excessive force to disperse demonstrators resulted in approximately 20 deaths; the opposition claimed at least 50 persons were killed. According to some reports, morgues were filled beyond capacity in the aftermath of the postelection violence.

b. Disappearance

There were numerous reports of disappearances.

On the night of August 31, heavily armed security forces, including republican guards and police, attacked the headquarters of opposition candidate Jean Ping. According to opposition leaders, two persons died, and many others were said to have disappeared. The government justified the attack by claiming criminals and weapons were being hidden at the headquarters.

c. Torture and Other Cruel, Inhuman, or Degrading Treatment or Punishment

The constitution prohibits torture and mistreatment of individuals, including prisoners. Security force personnel sometimes employed cruel and degrading treatment, however.

In September many sources reported the abuse of detainees arrested in the aftermath of the presidential election. A dual national with Gabonese citizenship claimed security forces beat him on the soles of his feet while he was in custody.

Refugees complained of harassment and extortion by security forces. According to reports from the African immigrant community, police and soldiers occasionally beat noncitizen Africans who lacked valid resident permits or identification. Authorities sometimes detained noncitizen Africans, ordered them to undress to humiliate them, and solicited bribes from them.

In December 2015, according to reliable international press sources, UN international peacekeeping troops, including from Gabon, allegedly took part in a prostitution ring in the M'Poko camp in the Central African Republic, paying 50 cents and $3 for sex with young girls. Government authorities investigated these cases but cleared those involved (in two cases, because the accuser mistook the flag of Rwanda on a soldier's uniform for the flag of Gabon). In September, however, four Gabonese peacekeepers were repatriated following a separate incident of alleged sexual exploitation. These cases were under investigation at year's end.

Prison and Detention Center Conditions

Prison conditions were harsh and potentially life threatening due to low quality food, inadequate sanitation, lack of ventilation, gross overcrowding, and poor medical care. Conditions in jails and detention centers mirrored those in prisons. There were no specific accommodations for persons with disabilities in prisons.

Physical Conditions: According to official statistics, there were 3,254 male and 119 female prisoners in the country's nine prisons at the end of 2015. Libreville's central prison was severely overcrowded; it was built to hold 500 inmates but held 2,014 at the end of 2015. Reports indicated overcrowding was also a problem in other prisons. The Director of Penal Affairs indicated there were three deaths in Libreville's prison. No other statistics were available.

In some cases authorities held pretrial detainees with convicted prisoners, juveniles with adults, and men with women. Authorities separated juvenile prisoners from adults in Libreville and Franceville prisons. There were separate holding areas within prisons for men and women, but access to each area was not fully secured or restricted. Prisoners had only limited access to food, lighting, sanitation, potable water, and exercise. On-site nurses were available to provide basic medical care, although prison clinics often lacked necessary medicines. For serious illnesses or injury, authorities transferred prisoners to public hospitals. Management of the spread of infectious diseases, such as HIV/AIDS and tuberculosis, was inadequate.

Administration: Prison authorities reported having received two complaints of inhuman conditions during the year. Observers believed the low incidence of complaints was due to ignorance of the process or a lack of faith in its effectiveness. There was no prison ombudsperson or comparable independent authority available to respond to prisoner complaints.

Independent Monitoring: The government permitted human rights organizations to conduct independent monitoring of prison conditions, but some reported difficulties in obtaining access to prisons. The International Committee of the Red Cross and the local NGO Malachie visited prisons.

d. Arbitrary Arrest or Detention

The constitution and law prohibit arbitrary arrest and detention, but the government did not always observe these prohibitions. Security forces arbitrarily arrested and detained irregular immigrants throughout the year. In the days prior to the presidential election and after the election results were announced, there were many arrests without warrants of opinion leaders in civil society and labor unions, as well as politicians in Libreville and Port-Gentil. Authorities subsequently charged or released those arrested.

Role of the Police and Security Apparatus

The national police, under the Ministry of Interior, and the gendarmerie, under the Ministry of Defense, are responsible for law enforcement and public security. Elements of the armed forces and the Republican Guard, an elite unit that protects the president under his direct authority, sometimes performed internal security functions. Civilian authorities maintained effective control over the national police, gendarmerie, republican guard, and all other branches of the security forces, and the government had mechanisms to investigate and punish those found responsible for abuse and corruption. Impunity was a significant problem, however.

Some police were inefficient and corrupt. Security force members sought bribes to supplement their salaries, often while stopping vehicles at legal roadblocks to check vehicle registration and identity papers. The Inspector General's Office was responsible for investigating police and security force abuse and corruption. No independent information regarding the effectiveness of this office was available.

Arrest Procedures and Treatment of Detainees

Although the law requires arrest warrants based on sufficient evidence and issued by a duly authorized official to make arrests, security forces in some cases disregarded these provisions. The law allows authorities to detain a suspect up to 48 hours without charge after which time the suspect must be brought before a judge to be charged. Police often failed to respect this time limit. Conditional release was possible after charges were filed if further investigation was required. There was a functioning bail system. Detainees were not always allowed prompt access to family members and a lawyer of their choice. The law requires the government provide indigent detainees with lawyers, but this was not always done, often because the government could not find lawyers willing to accept the terms of payment offered for taking such cases. Instances of these shortcomings spiked following the disputed presidential election. Except for the series of arrests made in the lead up to the election and in the days after the announcement of the outcome, arrests were made based on warrants issued by a judge or prosecutor based on evidence.

Authorities did not detain suspects incommunicado or hold them under house arrest. There were no reports detainees submitted complaints of abusive detention, but detainees generally lacked knowledge of their rights and the procedure for submitting complaints.

Arbitrary Arrest: Serge Mabiala, a prominent critic of the president and a leading figure of a dissent movement within the ruling PDG party, was arrested by intelligence service officers on charges of corruption and detained from September 16, 2015 until January 15. He was accused of embezzling approximately two billion CFA francs ($3.4 million) when he served as director of tax collection for large businesses in 2006-09. Authorities held him in Libreville's central prison and refused provisional release while he awaited a preliminary hearing. Mabiala's lawyers and family claimed authorities did not present a warrant at the time of his arrest, held him four days before officially bringing charges against him, and did not follow proper procedures for filing corruption charges. His supporters asserted these irregularities and the timing of his arrest--seven years after the alleged embezzlement and two months after he began speaking out against the government--were evidence his arrest was arbitrary and politically motivated. After his release, Mabiala had one hearing. At year's end the investigation continued.

Pretrial Detention: Prolonged pretrial detention was common due to overburdened dockets and an inefficient judicial system. The law limits pretrial detention to six months for a misdemeanor and one year for a felony charge, with six-month extensions if authorized by the examining magistrate. The law provides for a commission to deal with cases of abusive or excessive detention and grant compensation to victims, but the government had yet to establish such a commission. Approximately two-thirds of prison inmates were held in pretrial detention that could sometimes last up to three years. There were instances in which the length of pretrial detention exceeded the maximum sentence for the alleged crime. Although there were no reports detainees submitted complaints of abusive detention, detainees generally lacked knowledge of their rights and the procedure for submitting complaints, and may not have submitted complaints due to fear of retribution.

Detainee's Ability to Challenge Lawfulness of Detention before a Court: The law provides for detainees or persons arrested to challenge the legal basis and arbitrary nature of their detention. The law also provides for compensation if the court finds they were unlawfully detained. Authorities did not always respect these rights.

e. Denial of Fair Public Trial

The law provides for an independent judiciary, but the judiciary demonstrated only partial independence and only in some cases. The judiciary was inefficient and remained susceptible to government influence. The president appoints and may dismiss judges through the Ministry of Justice and Human Rights, to which the judiciary was accountable. In November magistrates went on strike, and one of their demands was for the removal of the head of state as the Magistrate Superior Council president. To address military cases, each year the Office of the Presidency appoints a military court composed of selected magistrates and military personnel. The military court provides the same basic legal rights as a civilian court. Outside the formal judicial system, minor disputes may be taken to a local traditional chief, particularly in rural areas, but the government did not always recognize such decisions. Corruption was a problem.

Authorities generally respected court orders.

Trial Procedures

The constitution provides for the right to a trial and to legal counsel, and the judiciary generally respected these rights. Trials were public. Trial dates were often delayed. In state security trials, the judge may deliver an immediate verdict of guilty at the initial hearing if the government presents sufficient evidence. Defendants have the right to a presumption of innocence. They have the right to be informed promptly and in detail of charges when booked at a police station, and authorities provided free interpretation as necessary, when staff members with the required language skills were available. A panel of three judges tries defendants, who enjoy the right to communicate with an attorney of choice and to adequate time and facilities to prepare their defense. Indigent defendants in both civil and criminal cases have the right to have an attorney provided at state expense, but the government often failed to provide attorneys because private attorneys refused to accept the terms of payment the government offered for such cases. Defendants have the right to confront witnesses against them, present witnesses or evidence on their behalf, access through their lawyer government-held evidence against them, and appeal. Defendants may not be compelled to testify or confess guilt. Defendants have the right to free interpretation as necessary from the moment charged through all appeals and have a right to be present at trial. The government generally extended these rights to all defendants.

Political Prisoners and Detainees

There were no reports of persons imprisoned solely for political reasons. There were, however, numerous reports of persons arrested during or after the disturbances that followed the disputed presidential election in August. Most of those arrested were soon released, or in some cases charged with ordinary criminal acts. Opposition and human rights advocates argued, however, these latter charges were politically motivated.

On September 23, gendarmes arrested without warrant Fefe Onanga, president of the Popular Radical Movement. Authorities did not present a warrant at the time of his arrest. On September 30, he was released on provisional liberty with charges of inciting violence. The case was under investigation at year's end.

On August 31, covert agency B2 forces (Direction Generale des Recherches) arrested a former PDG deputy who later joined the opposition. His lawyers and family claimed authorities did not present a warrant at the time of his arrest. The Secret Service held him 13 days before officially bringing charges against the defendant of criminal association, instigation of violence, and firearms possession. He denied all charges, denouncing his arrest as politically motivated and linked to his departure from the ruling party. The case against the defendant was pending at year's end and the defendant in pre-trial detention.

Civil Judicial Procedures and Remedies

Individuals and organizations may seek civil remedies for human rights violations through domestic courts. Persons seeking damages for, or cessation of, human rights violations may seek relief in the civil court system, although this seldom occurred.

Property Restitution

The government continued the practice of removing structures, including homes, it claimed were built on or infringed public property. The government asserted structures illegally built close to utilities and streets impeded traffic, violated zoning laws, and interfered with legal construction.

f. Arbitrary or Unlawful Interference with Privacy, Family, Home, or Correspondence

Although the constitution and law prohibit such actions, the government did not always respect these prohibitions. As part of criminal investigations, police requested and easily obtained search warrants from judges, sometimes after the fact. Security forces conducted warrantless searches for irregular immigrants and criminal suspects. Authorities also reportedly monitored private telephone conversations, personal mail, and the movement of citizens. Around the time of the presidential election, both opposition figures and international observers reported evidence of monitoring of their cell phones and other communications.

In September, after the announcement of the presidential election results, the Telecommunications Regulation Agency impeded cell phone texting with no explanation; the suspension was lifted on September 28.

Section 2. Respect for Civil Liberties, Including:

a. Freedom of Speech and Press

The constitution and law provide for freedom of speech and press, and the government generally respected these rights, although the government suspended one newspaper for one month and issued warnings to two others for publishing "defamatory" articles.

Press and Media Freedoms: Independent media were active and expressed a wide variety of views. The one major daily newspaper is affiliated with the government. Approximately 36 privately owned weekly or monthly newspapers represented independent views and those of political parties, but some appeared only irregularly due to financial constraints. All newspapers, including government-affiliated ones, criticized the government and political leaders of both opposition and progovernment parties. The country had both progovernment and opposition-affiliated broadcast media, although the main opposition-affiliated television station did not have the technical means to broadcast countrywide. According to the NGO Reporters without Borders, domestic law did not meet international standards on freedom of expression and media freedom.

<u>Violence and Harassment</u>: There were several reports of journalists being harassed and intimidated during the year.

For example, on July 23, gendarmes arrested and beat a journalist from French press agency Agence France-Presse. On September 10, authorities denied entry to the country to a journalist from the French publication *Le Monde Diplomatique.* Officials stated the journalist "lacked evidence on the length and the purpose of his stay."

During the night of August 31, masked gunmen attacked media outlet Radio Television Nazareth, owned by Pastor Bruno Ngoussi, a member of civil society, and set the station on fire.

<u>Censorship or Content Restrictions</u>: Most newspaper owners had either a progovernment or a pro-opposition political bias. Journalists at these newspapers practiced occasional self-censorship to placate owners.

<u>Libel/Slander Laws</u>: Libel and slander are treated as either a criminal offense or a civil matter. Editors and authors of articles ruled libelous in a court of law may be jailed for two to six months and fined 500,000 to five million CFA francs ($856 to $8,560). Penalties for libel, disrupting public order, and other offenses also include a one- to three-month publishing suspension for a first offense and a three- to six-month suspension for repeat offenses. The National Communication Council (CNC) advocated for the removal of criminal penalties for libel.

There was evidence that in several cases libel laws were applied to discourage or punish critical coverage of the government. For example, the CNC suspended two publications during the year. In June authorities fined newspaper *La Une* and suspended it for three months for criticizing the government. In September the CNC suspended opposition-leaning newspaper *Le Mbanja* for one month for printing an interview with an unnamed security official who alleged there were plans to kill anyone who disputed the president's reelection.

Internet Freedom

On August 30, following the disputed presidential election, the government blocked access to the internet and social media. On September 5, authorities re-established access to the internet for 12 hours a day but continued to block access to all social media sites. On September 29, full access to both the internet and social media was restored. The president stated in an interview on al-Jazeera the shutdown was a result of citizens having too many cell phones and "saturating" the internet.

According to the International Telecommunication Union 23.5 percent of the population used the internet in 2015.

Academic Freedom and Cultural Events

There were no government restrictions on academic freedom or cultural events.

b. Freedom of Peaceful Assembly and Association

Freedom of Assembly

The constitution and law provide for freedom of assembly, and for the first half of the year, the government generally respected this right. As the date for the presidential election approached, however, there were reports the government failed to approve permits for public meetings. Some civil society activists stated they did not submit requests to hold public meetings because they expected the government to deny them.

On July 23, police used tear gas to disperse an opposition-led rally of several hundred demonstrators calling for the president to resign. The organizers claimed the government did not respond to their request for a permit for the demonstration, so they decided to go ahead with it.

In September, following the presidential election, security forces significantly increased their presence in major towns, particularly parts of Libreville and Port-Gentil, as part of an effort to dissuade large groups from assembling.

c. Freedom of Religion

See the Department of State's *International Religious Freedom Report* at www.state.gov/religiousfreedomreport/.

d. Freedom of Movement, Internally Displaced Persons, Protection of Refugees, and Stateless Persons

The constitution and law provide for freedom of internal movement, foreign travel, emigration, and repatriation, and the government generally respected these rights.

The government cooperated with the Office of the United Nations High Commissioner for Refugees (UNHCR) and other humanitarian organizations in providing protection and assistance to refugees, returning refugees, asylum seekers, and other persons of concern. According to UNHCR, there were no known internally displaced persons or stateless persons in the country.

Abuse of Migrants, Refugees, and Stateless Persons: Despite efforts by the government and UNHCR to reduce discrimination, refugees complained of harassment and extortion by security force members. Some security force members harassed asylum seekers or refugees working as merchants, service sector employees, and manual laborers and, in order to extort bribes, refused to recognize valid documents held by refugees and asylum seekers. Many asylum seekers and refugees had expired documents and complained of administrative slowness to renew them, preventing these persons from working legally.

In-country Movement: Although there were no legal restrictions on internal movement, military and police personnel and gendarmes stopped travelers at checkpoints to check identity, residence, or registration documents and to solicit bribes. Refugees required a travel document endorsed by UNHCR and government authorities to circulate freely within the country.

Foreign Travel: The law requires a married woman to obtain her husband's permission to receive a passport and to travel abroad. The law prohibits individuals under criminal investigation from leaving the country. Refugees need a no-fee exit visa to leave from and return to the country, as do most holders of a residence permit. Exit visas were not issued promptly, which impeded persons' ability to depart.

On September 8, authorities prevented Louis Gaston Mayila, an opposition leader, from leaving the country. The government provided no explanation for its decision.

Protection of Refugees

Access to Asylum: The law provides for the granting of asylum or refugee status, and the government has established a system for providing protection to refugees. According to UNHCR, there were 913 refugees and 1,986 asylum seekers in the country.

The government's National Refugee Council and UNHCR conducted training sessions during the year on international law and the treatment of refugees for civil and military authorities.

Access to Basic Services: The law provided refugees equal access to public services, although there were reports that in some cases school and hospital employees improperly required refugees to pay additional fees. The National Health Insurance and Social Welfare Fund did not serve refugees.

Section 3. Freedom to Participate in the Political Process

The constitution and law provide citizens the ability to choose their government in free and fair periodic elections held by secret ballot and based on universal and equal suffrage. Secrecy of the ballot box is provided for by law and observed in practice. Citizens participated in regular presidential, legislative, and municipal elections. Members of the opposition questioned the fairness of the electoral process. The governing party has dominated all levels of government for nearly five decades. Members of the opposition urged the government to reinstate presidential term limits, replace the first-past-the-post system with a two-round voting system, reform the Constitutional Court, and create a more effective biometric voting program--measures opposition members believed would increase the fairness of the electoral system. These demands were a major theme in opposition demonstrations throughout the year.

Elections and Political Participation

Recent Elections: On August 31, National Electoral Commission (CENAP) announced the reelection of incumbent President and PDG candidate Ali Bongo Ondimba; the president won 50.7 percent of the vote, and leading opposition candidate Jean Ping received 47.2 percent. Voter turnout in the process, which was marred by irregularities, was 59.5 percent. Ali Bongo Ondimba was first elected in 2009, following the death of his father, president Omar Bongo, who died that year after a 41-year rule. International observers questioned the fairness of the vote, noting the president was credited with 95.5 percent of the vote in his home province on a turnout of 99.9 percent. Postelection violence (including the burning of the National Assembly building), significant lapses in respect for human rights, numerous arrests, and accusations of political tampering with the electoral process marred the election. Irregularities included problems with voter lists and registration, polls that opened late, improperly secured ballot boxes, organized proxy voting for members of the military, inconsistent application of rules regarding acceptable identification, and poorly trained poll workers. Authorities censored news coverage and harassed the press. Numerous candidates contested the election results, which the Constitutional Court nevertheless validated on September 23.

In the 2011 National Assembly elections, the PDG won 114 of 120 seats. Regional and local observers deemed the election generally free and fair despite minor irregularities. Observers estimated voter turnout at 34 percent. Opposition and civil society leaders had called for a boycott of these elections. The average turnout in legislative elections was approximately 40 percent.

In 2011 the minister of interior announced changes to the electoral code and the law governing political parties. Key changes included a reduction in the time permitted for revising the electoral list from 60 to 30 days and a decrease in the campaigning periods for legislative elections from 15 to 10 days. The reforms also give CENAP the authority to make decisions with a quorum of only four of the eight board members. Opposition leaders criticized these changes as limits on political participation, since the opposition selects only three of eight CENAP members; government officials or the PDG select the remaining five. They also stated that governing party politicians paid for votes and transported voters from other electoral districts to vote in their electoral districts.

The government introduced and employed biometric identification in voter registration in 2013. Opposition and civil society activists criticized the implementation process as inadequate to prevent fraud.

Political Parties and Political Participation: The PDG has dominated the government since its creation by former president Omar Bongo in 1968. PDG membership conferred advantage in obtaining government positions. Opposition members complained of unfair drawing of voter districts, alleging the president's home province received disproportionately more parliamentary seats than other provinces. They also stated that the PDG had greater access to government resources for campaign purposes than other parties.

In 2011 the government modified the law pertaining to political parties to prohibit leaders of dissolved political parties from forming new ones or serving on the board of an already existing party for five years after the party's dissolution. This modification occurred one month after the State Council upheld a court decision to dissolve the National Union Party (NUP) after party president and former interior minister Andre Mba Obame proclaimed himself the country's president in 2011.

In January 2015 the government reinstituted the NUP after significant lobbying by the international community and reversed the changes to the law prohibiting leaders of dissolved political parties from forming new ones. In August 2015 a NUP candidate won a special election to replace a national assembly member from the PDG who had resigned. During the year the NUP was active in an opposition coalition preparing to compete in presidential and legislative elections.

Participation of Women and Minorities: No laws prevent women or minorities from voting, running for office, or participating in politics. Some observers believed cultural and traditional factors prevented women from participating in political life to the same extent as men, however. Women held only four of 29 cabinet positions, 18 of 120 National Assembly seats, and only 18 of 102 Senate seats.

Members of all major ethnic groups occupied prominent government civilian and security force positions. Indigenous populations, however, rarely participated in the political process.

Section 4. Corruption and Lack of Transparency in Government

The law provides criminal penalties for corruption by officials, but the government did not implement the law effectively, and officials often engaged in corrupt practices with impunity. Some police were inefficient and corrupt. Security force members sought bribes to supplement their salaries, often while stopping vehicles at legal roadblocks to check vehicle registration and identity papers. The 2014 World Bank *Worldwide Governance Indicators* suggest corruption remained a serious problem.

In May 2015 the government officially launched a three-year Fight Against Corruption and Money Laundering strategy in partnership with the UN Development Program, National Commission against Illicit Enrichment (CNLCEI), National Agency for Financial Investigation, and private-sector and civil society partners. The strategy aims to encourage and reward ethical standards in public life, consolidate the rule of law, improve governance, increase transparency in the management of public finances, diminish inequality, and achieve a fair and transparent distribution of the benefits of growth.

<u>Corruption</u>: There were several prosecutions of public officials for alleged corruption during the year. In March, three Ministry of Agriculture, Husbandry, and Fishing civil servants were charged with embezzlement of 43 million CFA ($74,000). The accused were in jail awaiting trial at year's end.

<u>Financial Disclosure</u>: The law requires executive-level civil servants and civil servants who manage budgets to disclose their financial assets to the CNLCEI within three months of assuming office. Most officials complied, but some attempted to withhold information. The government did not make these declarations available to the public. There are administrative sanctions for noncompliance. According to the CNLCEI, it took steps to enforce the law during the year, including by deducting up to 100,000 CFA francs ($171) per month from the salaries of noncompliant civil servants or, in serious cases, by freezing their assets.

<u>Public Access to Information</u>: No law requires government offices to share information with the public. Individual offices may do so when requested, after assessing its sensitivity.

Section 5. Governmental Attitude Regarding International and Nongovernmental Investigation of Alleged Violations of Human Rights

A number of domestic human rights groups generally operated without government restriction, investigating and publishing their findings on human rights cases. During the period preceding the August presidential election as well as the postelection unrest, however, several human rights NGOs reported greater than usual governmental interference with their work and a general lack of responsiveness to their views.

<u>Government Human Rights Bodies</u>: In October the Ministry of Human Rights merged with the Ministry of Justice to create the Ministry of Justice and Human Rights. The ministry coordinates government efforts to improve respect for human rights, organize human rights training for government officials, and address major human rights problems. The National Human Rights Commission, composed of representatives from civil society, the media, the religious community, and the judiciary, has a degree of independence, although the government nominated its leadership and provided its funding. The commission acquired a headquarters in 2014 but lacked adequate funding and was not fully operational at year's end.

Section 6. Discrimination, Societal Abuses, and Trafficking in Persons

Women

<u>Rape and Domestic Violence</u>: The law criminalizes rape and provides penalties of five to 10 years' imprisonment for convicted rapists. Nevertheless, authorities seldom prosecuted rape cases. The law does not address spousal rape. There were no reliable statistics on the prevalence of rape, but a women's advocacy NGO estimated it to be a frequent occurrence. Discussing rape remained taboo, and women often opted not to report it due to shame or fear of reprisal. Only limited medical and legal assistance for rape victims was available.

Although the law prohibits domestic violence, NGOs reported it was common. Penalties for conviction range from two months' to 15 years' imprisonment. Women virtually never filed complaints, although the government operated a counseling group to provide support for abuse victims. An NGO operated a center to assist victims of domestic violence, and the government provided it with some in-kind support. Through the center's work, police intervened in response to some incidents of domestic violence.

<u>Female Genital Mutilation/Cutting (FGM/C)</u>: The law prohibits FGM/C, and there were no reports that it occurred.

<u>Sexual Harassment</u>: No law prohibits sexual harassment, and it remained a widespread problem. NGOs reported sexual harassment of women in the military was pervasive.

<u>Reproductive Rights</u>: Couples and individuals have the right to decide the number, spacing, and timing of their children, manage their reproductive health, and have access to the information and means to do so free from discrimination, coercion, and violence. Persons often lacked the information and means to do so, however. The UN Population Division estimated that only 21.9 percent of girls and women ages 15 to 49 used a modern method of contraception in 2015. The World Health Organization estimated the maternal mortality ratio to be 291 deaths for every 100,000 live births in 2015. The high maternal mortality ratio was attributed to the inadequate skills of health-care providers, lack of access to emergency obstetric care and family planning services, and high rates of adolescent pregnancy, estimated at 115 per 1,000 for girls and women ages 15 to 19. The Ministry of Health suggested the common practice of not seeking prenatal care also played a role.

<u>Discrimination</u>: Although the law does not generally distinguish between the legal status and rights of women and men, it requires a married woman to obtain her husband's permission to receive a passport and to travel abroad. No specific law requires equal pay for equal work. Women owned businesses and property, participated in politics, and worked in government and the private sector. Nevertheless, women faced considerable societal discrimination, including in obtaining loans and credit and, for married women, opening bank accounts without their husbands' permission and administering jointly owned assets, especially in rural areas.

Children

<u>Birth Registration</u>: Citizenship is conferred through one's parents and not by birth in the country. At least one parent must be a citizen to transmit citizenship. Registration of all births is mandatory, and children without birth certificates may not attend school or participate in most government-sponsored programs.

Many mothers could not obtain birth certificates for their children due to isolation in remote areas of the country or lack of understanding of the law.

<u>Education</u>: Although education is compulsory until age 16 and tuition-free through completion of high school, it often was unavailable after sixth grade in rural areas. Students were required to pay for their supplies, including school uniforms. The country had a shortage of classrooms and teachers.

<u>Child Abuse</u>: Child abuse occurred, but most cases were not reported, particularly if the abuse occurred within the family. When reports of abuse surfaced, police generally arrested the accused abusers, but an inefficient judicial system resulted in long delays in adjudication. A 2013 study by Samba Mwanas, a local NGO, reported abuse was common.

<u>Early and Forced Marriage</u>: The minimum age for consensual sex and marriage is age 15 for girls and 18 for boys. It was rare for girls under age 18 to marry but common for them to be in relationships with men outside of marriage. Teenage pregnancy was widespread.

<u>Female Genital Mutilation/Cutting (FGM/C)</u>: As reported in the section on women above, the law prohibits FGM/C, and there were no reports that it occurred.

<u>Sexual Exploitation of Children</u>: The law prohibits the commercial sexual

exploitation of children and child pornography, and authorities generally enforced the law. If convicted of procuring a child for prostitution or a child pornography-related offense, perpetrators may be sentenced to between two and five years' imprisonment. Child trafficking is punishable by imprisonment of up to 40 years and fines of up to 10 million to 20 million CFA francs ($17,123-$34.246); these penalties were sufficient to deter violations.

Some children were exploited in prostitution, but the problem was reportedly not widespread. The country was not known to be a destination for child sex tourism.

The law prohibits lewd pictures and photographs deemed "against the morals of society." The penalty for possession of pornography includes possible imprisonment from six months to one year and a fine of up to 222,000 CFA francs ($369).

International Child Abductions: The country is a party to the 1980 Hague Convention on the Civil Aspects of International Child Abduction. See the Department of State's *Annual Report on International Parental Child Abduction* at travel.state.gov/content/childabduction/en/legal/compliance.html.

Anti-Semitism

The Jewish population was very small, and there were no known reports of anti-Semitic acts.

Trafficking in Persons

See the Department of State's *Trafficking in Persons Report* at www.state.gov/j/tip/rls/tiprpt/.

Persons with Disabilities

The law prohibits discrimination against persons with "physical, mental, congenital, and accidental" disabilities and requires access to buildings and services, including voter access to election polling centers. Most public buildings, however, did not provide adequate access, hindering access to state services and the judicial system. The law subsumes sensory disabilities under congenital and "accidental" disabilities but does not recognize the concept of intellectual disability. The law provides for the rights of persons with disabilities to education, health care, and transportation. Enforcement was limited--there were no government programs to provide access to buildings, information, and communications for persons with disabilities. Children with disabilities generally attended school at all levels, including mainstream schools. Specialized schools provided education to some children with significant disabilities. There was access for persons with disabilities in air travel but not for ground transportation.

Societal discrimination occurred, and employment opportunities and treatment facilities for persons with disabilities were limited. Persons with disabilities faced barriers in obtaining employment, such as gaining access to human resources offices to apply for jobs, because buildings were not accessible. The inaccessibility of buses and taxis complicated seeking jobs or getting to places of employment for those without their own means of transportation.

Indigenous People

The Babongo, Baghama, Baka, Bakoya, and Barimba ethnic groups are the earliest known inhabitants of the country. Small numbers lived in large tracts of rainforest in the northeast. Most indigenous populations, however, were relocated to communities along the major roads during the late colonial and early post-independence periods. The law grants them the same civil rights as other citizens, but indigenous populations remained largely outside of formal authority, keeping their own traditions, independent communities, and local decision-making structures. They suffered societal discrimination, often lived in extreme poverty, and did not have easy access to public services. Discrimination in employment also occurred. Despite their equal status under the law, indigenous persons had little recourse if mistreated by persons from the majority Bantu population. No specific government programs or policies assisted them. According to the Movement for the Indigenous Minority known as Pygmies in Gabon, some members of this indigenous group have been able to vote for the first time, even without any targeted government policy to promote their inclusion.

Acts of Violence, Discrimination, and Other Abuses Based on Sexual Orientation and Gender Identity

The law does not criminalize sexual orientation or limit freedom of speech or peaceful assembly for lesbian, gay, bisexual, transgender, and intersex (LGBTI) persons. There are no specific antidiscrimination or hate crime laws, or other criminal justice mechanisms specifically designed to aid in the prosecution of bias-motivated crimes against members of the LGBTI community. There were no reports LGBTI persons were targeted for abuse, but underreporting of such incidents was likely, in view of societal stigma. Discrimination was a problem, however, and most LGBTI individuals chose to keep their status secret, except in trusted circles. Discrimination in employment and housing was a problem, particularly for LGBTI persons open regarding their sexual identity. Landlords often turned away such persons.

HIV and AIDS Social Stigma

Local NGOs reported discrimination against persons with HIV/AIDS. Persons with HIV/AIDS encountered difficulties obtaining loans and finding employment in at least some sectors. NGOs worked closely with the Ministry of Health to combat both the associated stigma and the spread of the disease.

Promotion of Acts of Discrimination

Some opposition politicians complained about what they contended was the excessive role of foreigners and citizens of non-Gabonese origin in the country's politics.

Ritual killings in which persons were killed and their limbs, genitals, or other organs amputated occurred and often went unpunished. The practice was driven by the belief that certain body parts have magical powers to enhance certain strengths. Blood was also used in rituals.

The local NGO Association to Fight Ritual Crimes reported 17 victims of ritual killings from January to October. The actual number of victims was probably higher. According to the association, many ritual killings were not reported or were incorrectly characterized. During the year authorities made no arrests of persons accused of ritual killing.

Section 7. Worker Rights

a. Freedom of Association and the Right to Collective Bargaining

The law protects the right of workers to form and join independent unions and bargain collectively. The law provides for the right to strike, with restrictions. Unions must register with the government to obtain official recognition, and the government routinely grants registration. The law provides for reinstatement for workers dismissed for union activities. Strikes may be called only after eight days' advance notification and only after arbitration fails. Public-sector employees are not allowed to strike based on the government claim their action could jeopardize public safety. The law does not define essential services sectors in which strikes are prohibited. The law prohibits government action against individual strikers who abide by the notification and arbitration provisions and excludes no groups from this protection. There are no special laws or exemptions from regular labor laws in the country's two export-processing zones. Although antiunion discrimination is illegal, some trade unionists in both the public and private sectors complained of occasional discrimination, including the blacklisting of union members, unfair dismissals, and threats to workers who unionized.

The government generally enforced applicable laws. Resources to protect the right to form unions, bargain collectively, and strike were adequate. Penalties for violations of these rights are compensatory and decided on a case-by-case basis and generally sufficient to deter violations. Administrative and judicial procedures were sometimes delayed.

Freedom of association and the right to collective bargaining generally were respected, and unions were generally not only politically active and influential but also independent of the government and political parties. Employers created and controlled some unions. Agreements negotiated by unions also applied to nonunion workers. Trade union representatives complained they experienced hurdles accessing educational establishments during their efforts to represent and defend their members' interests. Key labor union leaders noted the majority of labor violations stemmed from unwarranted dismissals, occasionally of workers on strike, leaving them without social security and insurance benefits, although there were no new labor violation cases during the year.

b. Prohibition of Forced or Compulsory Labor

The law prohibits forced or compulsory labor, including by children, but the penalties were not sufficiently stringent and did not reflect the serious nature of the offense. The law does not criminalize bonded labor. The government did not effectively enforce the law with respect to adult victims. The government enforced the law more actively to combat forced labor by children.

Resources, inspections, and remediation were inadequate. The lack of sufficient vehicles, budget, and personnel impeded the ability of labor inspectors to investigate allegations of forced labor. In addition labor inspectors found it difficult to access family-owned commercial farms and private households due to inadequate road infrastructure. The government did not strengthen the authority of labor inspectors during the year. The penalties for conviction of child trafficking were imprisonment for a maximum of 40 years and fines of up to 10 million to 20 million CFA francs ($17,123 to $34,247). These penalties were sufficient to deter violations.

Boys were subjected to forced labor as street hawkers or mechanics, as well as for work in handicraft shops. Boys and men were subjected to forced labor in agriculture, animal husbandry, fishing, and mining. Girls and women were exploited in domestic servitude, market vending, restaurants, and commercial sexual exploitation. Conditions included very low pay and forced long hours (see section 7.c.).

See also the Department of State's *Trafficking in Persons Report* at www.state.gov/j/tip/rls/tiprpt/.

c. Prohibition of Child Labor and Minimum Age for Employment

The law prohibits employment of children below age 16 without the express consent of the Ministries of Labor, Education, and Public Health. The law provides for fines from 290,000 to 480,000 CFA francs ($496 to $822) and prison sentences of up to two years for violations of the minimum age law. These penalties were sufficient to contribute to deterring violations.

The government effectively enforced the minimum age law in the formal sector. Authorities did not effectively enforce the law within the informal sector, however, primarily because the inspection force was inadequate.

The Ministry of Labor, Employment, Technical and Professional Training, and Youth Integration is responsible for receiving, investigating, and addressing child labor complaints through inspectors. The Interministerial Committee for the Fight against Child Trafficking is the mechanism for filing and responding to complaints. The committee drafted a 2015 Plan of Action for addressing exploitative child labor but had yet to implement it effectively. Complaints are referred to police, who carry out investigations and refer cases to the courts for prosecution. Although the Interministerial Committee has a network of approximately 2,000 persons to provide social services and support to victims of child labor at the local level, these individuals do not play an enforcement role.

During the year authorities removed at least 15 children from forced labor and arrested and prosecuted at least three individuals suspected of employing forced child labor.

Children sometimes were subjected to forced and exploitive labor. The government organized the repatriation of approximately four foreign children exploited in trafficking, and organized training sessions for authorities in charge to handle potential victims of trafficked children.

Child labor remained a problem. Noncitizen children were more likely than children of citizens to work in informal or illegal sectors of the economy, where laws against child labor were seldom enforced. An unknown number of children, primarily noncitizens, worked in marketplaces or performed domestic labor. Many of these children were the victims of child trafficking (see section 7.b.). Citizen children, particularly street children, also worked in the informal sector.

Child laborers generally did not attend school, received only limited medical attention, and often experienced exploitation by employers or foster families. In an effort to curb the problem, police often fined the parents of children who were not in school. Laws forbidding child labor covered these children, but abuses often were not reported.

See the Department of Labor's *Findings on the Worst Forms of Child Labor* at www.dol.gov/ilab/reports/child-labor/findings/.

d. Discrimination with Respect to Employment and Occupation

The labor code prohibits discrimination regarding employment and work conditions based on race, color, sex, religion, political opinion, disability, national origin or citizenship, or social background. It does not address discrimination based on sexual orientation, gender identity, age or language. The government did not effectively enforce this law. No specific law requires equal pay for equal work. Discrimination in employment occurred with respect to indigenous persons, persons with HIV/AIDS, and LGBTI persons. There were reports of labor exploitation of indigenous persons by their Bantu neighbors, who paid them much less than the minimum wage.

e. Acceptable Conditions of Work

The national monthly minimum wage was 150,000 CFA francs ($257).

Government workers received an additional monthly allowance of 20,000 CFA francs ($34) per child and transportation, housing, and family benefits. There was no minimum wage in the informal sector. A 2013 government-commissioned report on poverty defined the poverty income level at 80,000 CFA francs ($137) per month per family.

The labor code stipulates a 40-hour workweek with a minimum rest period of 48 consecutive hours. The law also provides for paid annual holidays. Employers must compensate workers for overtime work as determined by collective agreements or government regulations. According to the law, the daily limit for compulsory overtime may be extended from 30 minutes to two hours to perform specified preparatory or complementary work, such as starting machines in a factory or supervising a workplace. It also may be extended for urgent work to prevent or repair damage from accidents. The daily limit does not apply to establishments in which work is continuous or to establishments providing retail, transport, dock work, hotel and catering services, housekeeping, security services, medical establishments, domestic work, and journalism.

The Ministry of Health establishes occupational safety and health standards. The Ministry of Labor is responsible for enforcing minimum wage, overtime, and safety and health standards in the formal sector. Employers generally respected minimum wage standards. Formal sector employees could submit complaints regarding overtime or health and safety standards, and the ministry's labor inspectors investigated such complaints. The government penalized violations with a range of fines that contributed to deterring violations. In the formal sector, workers may remove themselves from situations that endanger health or safety without jeopardy to their employment, and authorities effectively protected employees in the formal sector in this situation.

The government did not enforce labor code provisions in the informal economy, or in sectors where the majority of the labor force was foreign, such as in the mining and timber sectors. Employers obliged foreign workers to work under substandard conditions, dismissed them without notice or recourse, and often physically mistreated them. Employers frequently paid noncitizens less than citizens and required them to work longer hours, often hiring them on a short-term, casual basis to avoid paying taxes, social security contributions, and other benefits.

www.ingramcontent.com/pod-product-compliance
Lightning Source LLC
Chambersburg PA
CBHW081259250726
48654CB00012B/1662